THE PACIFIC NORTHWEST POETRY SERIES

Linda Bierds, *General Editor*

THE PACIFIC NORTHWEST POETRY SERIES

2001 John Haines *For the Century's End*

2002 Suzanne Paola *The Lives of the Saints*

2003 David Biespiel *Wild Civility*

2004 Christopher Howell *Light's Ladder*

2005 Katrina Roberts *The Quick*

2006 Bruce Beasley *The Corpse Flower*

2007 Nance Van Winckel *No Starling*

2008 John Witte *Second Nature*

2009 David Biespiel *The Book of Men and Women*

2010 Christopher Howell *Dreamless and Possible*

2011 Katrina Roberts *Underdog*

2012 Kathleen Flenniken *Plume*

PLUME

Plume, the twelfth volume in the Pacific Northwest Poetry Series, is published with the generous support of Cynthia Lovelace Sears.

UNIVERSITY OF WASHINGTON PRESS
PO BOX 50096, SEATTLE, WA 98145, USA
WWW.WASHINGTON.EDU/UWPRESS

LIBRARY OF CONGRESS CATALOGING-IN-PUBLICATION DATA
Flenniken, Kathleen.
Plume : poems / by Kathleen Flenniken.
      p. cm.
Includes bibliographical references.
ISBN 978-0-295-99153-5 (cloth : alk. paper)
I. Title.
ps3606.l47p58 2012
811'.6—dc22   2011030371

The paper used in this publication is acid-free and meets the minimum requirements of American National Standard for Information Sciences— Permanence of Paper for Printed Library Materials, ANSI z39.48–1984.∞

Printed and bound in the United States of America
Designed by Ashley Saleeba

Endpapers: Hanford Site, Declassified Documents Retrieval System, NID0052475; scanned from original by Richland Operations Office, Department of Energy.
p. 2: Site diagram of Hanford Engineer Works (from Henry DeWolf Smyth, *Atomic Energy for Military Purposes* [Princeton University Press, 1945])

For Carolyn

and in memory of her father
T. J. Deen (1929–1988)

and mine
R. L. Dillon (1920–2001)

. . . But he found it too much for his discretion to keep such a secret; so he went out into the meadow, dug a hole in the ground, and stooping down, whispered the story, and covered it up. Before long a thick bed of reeds sprang up in the meadow and as soon as it had gained its growth, began whispering the story, and has continued to do so, from that day to this, every time a breeze passes over the place.

—the barber from the story of Midas, *Bulfinch's Mythology*

CONTENTS

PLUME

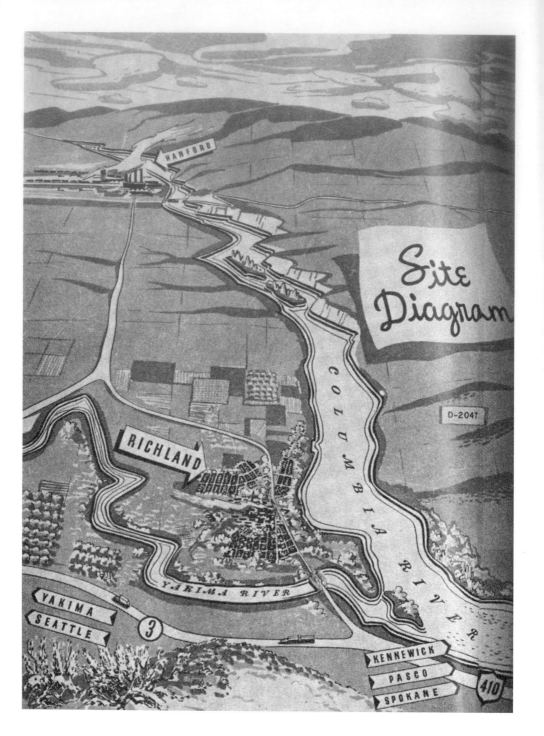

CAMPAIGN Q&A, SOMEWHERE IN OREGON, MAY 18, 2008

WOMAN IN AUDIENCE: *Every year the government promises to fund the Hanford cleanup project in eastern Washington, and every year they find a way to take away the funding, which results in a lot of lost jobs. Washington's current policy seems to be, "The solution to pollution is dilution."*

BARACK OBAMA: *Oh. Nice.*

WOMAN: *What is your policy?*

OBAMA: *Here's something you'll rarely hear from a politician, and that is, I'm not familiar with the Hanford Site. And so I don't know exactly what's going on there. Now, having said that, having said that, I promise you I'll learn about it by the time I leave here on the ride back to the airport.*

MY EARLIEST MEMORY PRESERVED ON FILM

—John Kennedy at Hanford Nuclear Reservation, September 26, 1963

Somewhere in that sea of crisp white shirts
    I'm sitting on my father's shoulders
as you dedicate our new reactor and praise us

for shaping history. The helicopter that set you down
    in our proudest moment
waits camera right, ready to whisk you away.

A half century later, I click play again and again
    for proof you approve—
but the nuclear age is complicated.

Are you amazed that eight reactors
    mark the bend in our river?
Are you troubled we need a ninth? I can't forget

we'll lose you in a few weeks, that sometime
    between then and now
our presidents will forget us.

But today the wind is at your back, like a blessing.
    Our long-dead senators applaud
as you touch a uranium-tipped baton to a circuit

and activate a shovel atomically.
    This is the future.
Dad holds me up to see it coming.

RATTLESNAKE MOUNTAIN

We claim it's the tallest treeless mountain
in the world, which is only true
if you behold it—

mistress of dust storms, wildfires,
windswept and monochrome—and acknowledge
we live exposed to the planets here,

that the mountain's folds and shadows
roll with stars, soft April greens, and lupine,
belying missile silos hidden in catacombs

and the waste of 50 years of atomic bombs.
Our families all came from elsewhere,
and regarded the desert as empty,

and ugly, which gave us permission
to savage the land. The mountain,
figure in repose, looked on

as we buried what we buried at its hem.
Desert turned vineyard, orchard, strip mall,
houses in every shade of beige.

This radioactive burial ground
and the hills along its edge are the last
unbroken stretch of shrub-steppe remaining.

I left the mountain half my life ago
to live among trees,
and now—an exile—I understand

what beautiful ghost rises up in the distance
in my dreams. Now I know
this ruined place is sacred.

MAP OF CHILDHOOD

I

on this street designed by idealists
neighbors lead parallel lives
though at work

one wears ties   one whites

one calculates exposure   one is exposed
                              his body bombarded
                              and no use holding
                              his breath

but otherwise share
a drill   lawn edger   backyard fence

II

in this map of childhood
my house and Carolyn's house are identical
separated by three identical houses
and the intersection of Cottonwood Drive and Cedar Avenue

if you lift off our roofs and peer inside
our lives are mirror images
her brothers sleep in my parents' room
my brothers sleep in her parents' room
and Carolyn's room and my room are the same

and here
exactly where I am pointing
she and I eat snowflakes
as we walk each other home halfway

A GREAT PHYSICIST RECALLS THE MANHATTAN PROJECT

—John A. Wheeler (1911–2008)

Think of our little group with a map spread out in front of us—
great expanses of the empty west—as if we were new Columbuses.

Think of it—a *desert* in Washington State. Along the icy blue Columbia.
Think of the caravan of laborers, several hundred a night, unloading at Pasco.

Immense mess halls accommodating thousands. Big band dances.
Beer joints with ground-level windows for tear gas. Constant construction.

When the chain reaction at B Reactor died that first night,
the mood was excitement and puzzlement. As for whether

I solved the poisoning riddle, let no man be his own judge.
Fermi was there. A marvelous person. One scorching Sunday afternoon,

our group hiked along a rushing irrigation canal. If we jumped in,
how would we get out? Fermi thought our ropes were sissy. The water

dragged him downstream clambering, until he reappeared,
roughed up, shins bleeding. That was Fermi. That's how he got things done.

I recall a Sunday with the children hiking in the Horse Heaven Hills.
I watched my youngest climb as the sun blazed behind her golden hair

and realized that halos were not a painter's invention,
but a consequence of nature. Have you ever held plutonium

in your hand? Someone once gave me a piece shaped and nickel-plated
so alpha particles couldn't reach the skin. It was the temperature, you see,

the element producing heat to keep itself warm—not for ten
or a hundred years, but thousands of years. This is the energy contained

in Hanford's fuel. I think of that place as a song not properly sung.
A romantic song. And not one person in a hundred knows the tune.

BEDROOM COMMUNITY

We were all bedded down
in our nightcaps, curtains drawn

as swamp coolers and sprinklers
hissed every brown summer hour, or in winter

sagebrush hardened in the cold. It was still dark
as our fathers rose, dressed, and boarded

blue buses that pulled away, and turn
in milk trucks came collecting bottled urine

from our doorsteps. Beyond the shelter belt
of Russian olive trees, cargo trains shuffled past

at 8:00 and 8:00, and the wide
Columbia rolled by, silent with walleye

and steelhead. We pulled up our covers
while our overburdened fathers

dragged home to fix a drink,
and some of them grew sick—

Carolyn, your father's marrow
testified. Whistles from the train,

the buses came, our fathers left.
Oh Carolyn—while the rest of us slept.

DOCUMENT CONTROL

Begin please with a bird's eye view.

Circa 1945. A report (not legible up here) is carefully typed,
in another room reviewed, and in another room
classified [SECRET], document number assigned, and filed
(we observe the librarian's bald spot).
Repeat.
Repeat.
Repeated thousands of times.

Where are we now?

Reports are rolling off typewriters sixty years ago,
ready to be checked by peers. There are managers
who manage managers who manage meetings
to review reviews of secret documents like these.

What kind of information do these documents contain?

Some nights workers return to their freshly built
identical houses, drop their boots, badges,
and change, don't know they're misplaced
until their next door neighbors' wives
call them honey from another room.
We don't know what the documents contain.

But how can we claim them? How can we find out?

Somewhere else, a decade later, back row,
a girl in a Peter Pan collar sounds out words
in a Dick and Jane reader. She will play her role.
We are all dependent on what each of us knows.

MOSQUITO TRUCK

Come in now, come in, my father commanded, hearing its slow progress up Cottonwood Drive, even if this were one of those fine evenings that seemed to last into tomorrow, one of those fine evenings every kid on the street was out on a banana-seat bike, or dribbling a basketball, or still wet in a swimsuit and running in the yard. And the aluminum sashes tight in their frames announced we were slamming our windows to the entire neighborhood, which made it worse somehow, to be publicly stuck inside while the rumbling approached like an army of liberators, then the truck itself with its glorious spray and billowing sweet-smelling chemical clouds, its pea-soup fog. All the kids but us rode and ran along behind, those flashy sting rays with their tasseled handlebars, little towheads and big brothers who whooped and hollered, breathing deep and willing themselves not to cough, who pulled wheelies and pinwheels as if they were rodeo stars in a parade. Which this was. The driver, as benevolent as if he were dispensing ice cream, waved and grinned into his side view mirror. Hello, hello! What summer entertainment! *Damned kids,* my father would say, shaking his head and probably right.

HERB PARKER FEELS LIKE DANCING

—Richland, 1949

Mr. Parker's Sunbeam is shiny as an atom.
He pulls up, alights with grace
and makes his dance hall entrance.
Perhaps you sense his English accent
and pocket square. Women shy
like ponies to one corner. He corrals one
and trots her around the dance floor.

Herb Parker rides a shapely 4/4.
"That Old Black Magic,"
"Baby, It's Cold Outside."
Maybe it is, or maybe it's blazing,
unsafe to breathe tonight.

Her earrings are zircon daisies.
A silver belt rings her slim waist.
Herb Parker steers her toward
his dark place. "Mr. Parker?"
he hears somebody ask, like a tremble
on a seismograph, but you can't blame
Herbert Parker for his appetites.

He palms the tender center of
her back. "Mr. Parker?" again.
Perhaps it's her voice, or her husband's,
or one of the voices in his head. He's
a Dutch master with his finger in the dike,
a valvular, crepuscular figure.

"Look out the window at that storm . . ."
He takes the government's calls
and negotiates those devil's bargains,
how much of their order can he fill?

You understand they say "product"
and mean plutonium, they mean
how many bombs can you afford to fuel?
"Darling, down and down I go,

round and round I go in a spin" . . .
the river, and its sediments,
the air, capricious with winds,
the soil column, the ground water,
the vase of wildflowers on Deputy Chief
Gamertsfelder's desk! Native species
sprouting in Richland yards.
The mosquitoes, for pity's sake,
the farm animals, the farmers living
off the land, the water birds and the
duck hunters, the bottom fish and
the fishermen on Richland dock.
Everything he thinks to test . . . good god,

the entire food chain contaminated.
He's basically a shy man with
immeasurable power. A sultan
coaxing his courtesan's smile.
She only shakes a little now.
Don't you understand? *Someone*
must step forward and play God.
How much better that the man
can lead? hold you tight
in his very good hands, and spin.

RICHLAND DOCK, 2006

The Columbia rolls on
through the desert,
unimpressed and unattached—
a woman who doesn't need boys
to dance, a king's parade
of golden carriages,
an endless line of warrior ants.
The river speaks French
in a land of inferior grammar.
The river is blue in a field of brown,
green in a field of gray,
black in a field of bronze.
The river shuns the desert.
It holds its tongue.
It saves itself for the ocean.
The river is fast, undammed,
Rapunzel's hair let down,
and won't allow this
shrub-steppe plain to climb it.
The river won't lend itself
to grow a tree. Look—
sagebrush flush with its banks.
No meeting, no kiss, no marriage.
Look at the tumbleweeds.
The river bathes in its glory,
the desert eats dust. The river
belongs to somewhere else.
The mighty river passes, not touching.
But not untouched.

DAYS OF CLOTHESLINES

Mother pinned laundry to the backyard breeze
while Mrs. Mumford's voice darted over the tall fence,

plum to pear and back, like a bird. Her accent
deeply southern. Her face obstructed

and forgotten, so substitute the pushed-in features
of her boxer dog, Sue. Our family sheets

breathed in and out while Mrs. Mumford's voice insisted
cancer, cancer, as if calling it home. Her doctors couldn't find it.

Sue looked mean, but loved to be patted through the slats.
Mother named these monologues *getting caught for hours.*

Mr. Mumford already dead, and his widow listed off
other neighbors with cancer too. Cancer in the air,

cancer everywhere. Flopped down in the grass,
face up, I searched the clouds, wagons ho,

migrating left to right. Billowing abandoned laundry.
Doctors, given chance after chance, finally discovered

Mrs. Mumford was right. She brought the news to Mother
formally, in our living room, dressed up

with the best grammar she could find.
The whites of remembered laundry are blue white.

She willed it, Mother used to say. Sue was a sweet dog,
but unforgivably ugly. Even as I petted her, I didn't want to.

WHOLE-BODY COUNTER, MARCUS WHITMAN ELEMENTARY

"The mobility of this new laboratory provides versatile capabilities for measuring internally deposited gamma-ray-emitting radionuclides in human beings." —Health Physics, November 1965

We were told to close our eyes.
Everyone was school age now, our
kindergarten teacher reminded us,

old enough to follow directions
and do a little for our country.
My turn came and the scientists

strapped me in and a steady voice
prompted, The counter won't hurt,
lie perfectly still, and mostly I did

and imagined what children
pretend America is, parks
bordered by feathery evergreens,

lawns so green and lush
they soothe the eyes, and pupils
open like love—

a whole country of lawns
like that. Just once I peeked
and the machine had taken me in

like a spaceship and I moved
slow as the sun through the chamber's
smooth steel sky.

I shut my eyes again and pledged
to be still; so proud to be
a girl America could count on.

PLUME

For   years
it   may   be   locked
in   the   matrix
of   silt   and   sand
like   a   photo-
graphic   image
still   and
untransported
absorbed
and   adsorbed
then
the   introduction
of   gradient
to   unsaturated
soils

                    percolation
and   it   awakens
unfurling
like   a   frond
a   carpet   unrolling
itself

                    remote
                    underground
this   beautiful
movement
fanning
between   interstices
feathering
void   to   void
describes
the   dark   earth
the   layering
of   permeable
and   impermeable
soils

it   is   out
of   our   hands
this   50   year   old
mistake
this   poison
yes   it   is   moving
to   the   river   yes
it   migrates
between   grains
down   to
saturated   sediment
manifestly   down
and   when
it   descends
as   far   as   it   can
it   will   swim
ride   droplets
like   swanboats
float
spread

                         diffuse
                         distend
trailing   its
delicate
paisley   scarf
and   like
anything
with   a   destiny
a   flock   of   birds
sperm
                         breath
it   will   move
downstream
to   the   river
yes   the   river
will   take   it   in

TO CAROLYN'S FATHER

—Thomas Jerry Deen, 1929–1988

On the morning I got plucked out of third grade
    by Principal Wellman because I'd written on command
an impassioned letter for the life of our nuclear plants
    that the government threatened to shut down
and I put on my rabbit-trimmed green plaid coat
    because it was cold and I'd be on the televised news
overseeing delivery of several hundred pounds of mail
    onto an airplane bound for Washington DC addressed
to President Nixon who obviously didn't care about your job

    at the same time inside your marrow
blood cells began to err one moment efficient the next
    a few gone wrong stunned by exposure to radiation
as you milled uranium into slugs or swabbed down
    train cars or reported to B Reactor for a quick run-in-
run-out and by that morning Mr. Deen
    the poisoning of your blood had already begun

AFTERNOON'S WIDE HORIZON

That mushroom cloud filling
my cousins' color TV stained orange
what remained black and white at home.
The atomic age had been a fond friend
where I lived in Atomic City. The atom
had something to do with
who I was. Now
the sky on screen filled with fire.
What is that, I asked.

What is that, I asked
the sky on screen filled with fire.
Who I was now
had something to do with
where I lived, in Atomic City. The atom,
the atomic age, had been a fond friend.
What remained black and white at home?
My cousins' color TV stained orange,
that mushroom cloud filling
afternoon's wide horizon.

The dissemination of scientific and technical information relating to atomic energy should be permitted and encouraged so as to provide that free interchange of ideas and criticisms which is essential to scientific progress.—The Atomic Energy Act of 1946

REDACTION I

GREEN RUN

—Hanford, Washington, December 2, 1949

Green

        a verdant dream

                grass avenues framed by trees

Green

        untested

            young

Run

        as in long limbs racing

Green as in raw

          uncured

             uranium slugs

                 aged 16 days instead of 90

Run

        meaning *batch*

             an 8,000 curie brew

or *Green*

        lush with buds

            or with radioiodine 131

                dead night

                  stack a-belching

                when the weather turns

                  to snow

Run as in production

        fallout

             over thousands of square miles

Green as in *sickly*

        taken up

            by the thyroid

Run as in *hide*

        as in *keep the lid on this disaster*

Run as in *spill*

                as out of a cauldron

Green

            meaning

                  easily deceived

                            meaning

                                  run

BIRD'S EYE VIEW

Let's return to our perch on a cloud.
Perhaps a pattern is discernible in our town.

You can observe from here
that certain thoughts are eliminated
at the source. A dichotomy results,
permitting complex scientific research
and acceptance of delivered truth.

We would never foul our own nest.

Never. As a last resort.
Only inside the nuclear reservation.
Occasionally entrained sediments.
Or where the water table
lies hundreds of feet below ground.
Or effluent if particulates settle
near the source. Perhaps bottom fish
if fishermen throw them back.
Local livestock if the public
is informed that trucked-in milk
is pasteurized and preferred.
If land north of Richland closes
for hunting, "Too crowded to be safe."
If harmless-sounding press releases
are filed. "We recommend that you
use iodized salt." If aggressive
insect control ensues. And those men
in your pasture, those men in white
holding instruments to your grass
and cows, who run when they see you
coming, jump in their trucks
and disappear—they are monitoring
pollen. It's nothing, rest assured.

Your expression has changed.

One half of my brain
is giving the other half a beating.

I know. I know.

RICHLAND DOCK, 1956

Someone launched a boat into the current,

caught and delivered fish to the lab
and someone tested for beta and P-32.
Someone with flasks and test tubes tested
and re-tested to double check the rising values.

And someone drove to the public dock
with a clipboard and tallied species and weight.
Chatting with his neighbors, *Which fish
are you keeping? How many do you eat?*

And someone with a slide rule in a pool of light
figured and refigured the radionuclide
dose. Too high. Experimented frying up
hot whitefish. No. No. Then someone decided

all the numbers were wrong. Someone
from our town. Is that why we
were never told? While someone fishing—
that little boy; the teacher on Cedar Street—

caught his limit and never knew.

ON COTTONWOOD DRIVE

In this story my brother is four
and sleepwalks out our front door
into the dark lawn in his nightgown

(in truth he woke lifting the latch—
our family stories mostly abort
before they're begun)

but in this story he wanders into a fight—
Mr. Mumford next door in chasing
his son Spenser with an axe

(it was years later and he watched
from the window—we sometimes wagered
which Mumford would get murdered)

but in this story my father wakes
at the sound of the opening lock
and blunders into this scalp hunt

(the Mumfords took their fight inside
and mister sank his axe
in Spenser's bedroom wall)

In truth I like this version
of two versions of the truth combined
because it tells how close we lived

SELF-PORTRAIT WITH FATHER AS TOUR GUIDE

You're eighteen. It's August brim to brim
and your father is at the wheel. He points proudly
at distant reactors and spires, sun-baked highway

and barbed wire, and offers them to you.
You've waited all your life.
A gate patrolman waves you across the threshold

into the Cold War world. You grew up downstream,
sugared by these winds, while Dad
and Carolyn's Dad and every father you knew

disappeared to fuel the bomb. He drives you
past canyon buildings like grounded ocean freighters.
A dozen miles more and White Bluffs shimmers

into view—a ghost town with your very own eyes,
the shell of old Hanford High School,
sad remnants of abandoned farms. Dad is pointing,

but wind and speed carry his voice away. . . .

Look at me, trying to retrieve him
across three decades. Kathleen—girl-I-used-to-be—
enjoy your afternoon, flash your one-day badge

at jack rabbits and coyotes. If he's dead now,
if all the fathers will soon be dead,
know they made their mark. They'll matter for centuries.

INTERLUDE FOR DANCERS

—Richland, 1969

A somersaulting boy
plays a tumbleweed
while three ballerinas dance
their role as the wind—
hair loose, skirts thick,
their crinolines caked
with dust. Remember?
we say in the audience,
elbowing each other.
Remember sand
in our eyes and mouths,
residents quitting in droves
blown out of town by gusts
we called *termination?*
Leather-soled
government men step out
to pas-de-deux with our
dust storms, who extend
en pointe and pirouette,
their eyes finely lashed
and batting back grit
against a backdrop of brown
Horse Heaven Hills.
How beautiful! we might say
or anyway, How tragic!
as the men attend
and the prickly boy
tumbles and clowns.
The hometown girls
make good—they billow
and blast, ripple like flags,
and lob loose clods
of earth. Look at them. . . .

Look at what art we make!
But what the wind blows in,
it blows along.
And we are what's left.

The whole point of science is . . . to invite the detection of error and to welcome it. . . . To keep completely secret the design of the Hanford piles I think has never been a controversial thing. To keep secret the fact that we don't know how to do some things may be controversial because it may be that we really need some ideas, and the classification, or keeping secret, our ignorance of an area in which we haven't been able to make any progress may in some cases be a very serious hindrance to getting the insight, the bright ideas and the progress which would come if a much wider group of people could be interested.

—J. Robert Oppenheimer, 1947

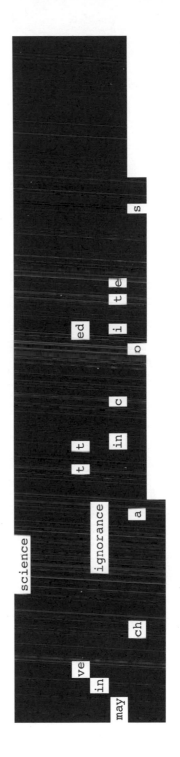

AUGEAN SUITE

I. The Fifth Labor of Hercules

Augeus's vast herds of cattle were divine
but their shit was earthly,
and divinely abundant.

The stench hung over the valley,
palpable. Nobody
waded into the fouled stable

without drowning.
This gave Hercules his idea
to divert two rivers,

the Alpheus and the Peneus,
and sluice the filth away,
which he finished in a single day.

Then he slew King Augeus
to remind us the world belongs
to gods and kings,

that exacting justice is worthier
than atoning for sins.
No more mention

of the two gangrenous rivers,
the women downstream washing clothes
or their children bathing.

II. Augean Gray, 1954

Flakes emitted from the process stack
could be discerned by the eye
the way one might hear the taps
of countless leather soles
treading a busy bus lot
and yet not *attend* them—

not notice their drift and fall.
Say the click of my mother's heels
as she pushed one baby in a carriage
and pulled another by the hand
through the nearby village in August—
as it snowed radioruthenium.
She wouldn't know to listen.

If only she'd thought to ask
why snow fell that summer.
If only the villagers had asked
why 17,000 signs were erected
all over the desert to
Keep Off the Grass.

III. Internal Report, Herbert M. Parker, 1954

One can picture the entire population of Richland lying unclothed on the ground for one day. There would be about 25 identifiable particles in contact with skin; not more than three would be in an activity type range that could produce a significant effect; not more than one would probably produce an effect. . . . At the worst, there would be a small necrotic area, perhaps comparable with the effect of plunging a lighted match head to the skin. My best guess is that this would not happen in one day's contact with the hottest known offsite particle. . . . Pig skin and human skin are sufficiently alike that if the pig can wear a 400 mrad/hr particle for five days, I would be willing to wear one for one day.

IV. Augean Gray

Women,
      take off your
            dresses
                  and undergarments.
        You babies,
              crawl naked
     in the grass.
           Lie down all of you

     under the August sky,

                and nobody ask
                    Questions alarm
and weaken
         our nation.

It is snowing.

    Your men are at work   making snow.

          I will go first   and close my eyes,

      cross the distance

             between here

                    and winter.

    Lie down, patriot.

            Don't ask.

V. The Graying of Herbert Parker, 1956

There will be through the course of the years
a very slow build-up, he said.
One knows the final answer only some 10,
20, or 30 years from now. He said, *Perhaps*
by the time the deposit becomes a hazard
the true permissible levels will be known,
and the word *permissible* was downy
as fine snow. *It is rather easy to show,* he said,
an undesirable tendency to concentrate where
least desired. As though Jack Frost had touched
his mind. *The obvious hazard is not always—*
flakes started falling in earnest—*one might*
almost dare to say not usually—the real hazard.
While snow drifted behind his eyes.

VI. Herbert Parker's Statement to Congress, 1962

MR. PARKER: *If we accept the principle of acceptable risk in radiation exposure, and there is no alternative today, instead of black and white, we have only infinite gradation of gray from perhaps a black relating to significant over-exposure, grading down but never reaching white. It is beyond our wits to quantify such a scale. Yet the attempt has to be made at least to define bands of gray. The three ranges as used by the Federal Radiation Council, I think, are precisely such an attempt which I have translated into fashionable color terminology with range I being Arcadian gray, range II being Achillean gray, and range III being Augean gray.*

REPRESENTATIVE HOSMER: *Do you have a color chart with you?*

MR. PARKER: *I am not able to put precise numbers on these shades of gray but I classify Arcadian gray as pure and clean for the relevant purpose, and Augean gray containing a reference to the well-known stables of history, and the middle range, if I may clarify that, as I recall Achilles, he was pretty sound but he had a couple of weak spots, one on each heel.*

SIREN RECOGNITION

—Hanford, 1983

The orientation video begins with fire
and hurricane—familiar, comfortable disaster.
Then, with a queer segue, the *AWOOGA*
AWOOGA of commencing reactor meltdown.

I sit in my summer suit from Nordstrom,
the only new hire today, not dressed
for fear in the shape of a mushroom cloud
or the end of the human race.

The clerk sorts through papers as though
this is any work day. I believe in her
eye shadow, the orange on her desk,
but the siren sounds deep in my lizard brain,

in my involuntary heart which has
stopped and locked—the way security
(explains a calm voice in the video)
will lock down the gates and my chicken body

run in circles as my severed future fries.
Hear the siren once and it will change
your life. That night I'll wake transformed
into a cockroach, scaling the inside

of a reactor dome.

HAND AND FOOT COUNT

—Workers returning from the field
will self-check for radiation contamination
using the Hand and Foot Monitor.

I'm all crapped up
Bong bong bong
Come two rad techs in a dead run

I'm freeze-tagged
Popcorn on the Geiger counter
Hot and ready for melted butter

They peel me off the ceiling
and scrub me down fast
with nothing but elbow grease and company Kotex

They soothe me
dressed in whites and masks
rubbing me up like cats

Patted and cooed and screened clean
dusted off and grinning
collar straight and on my merry way

I'm standing out with the tumbleweeds
on a brash blue day
Locked inside a razor-wire electric fence

What next?

ATOMIC MAN

*—After a 1976 Hanford industrial explosion, Harold McCluskey, 64,
was kept in isolation for five months to prevent exposing others.*

One look at me and you'd guess
the laboratory accident—a thousand-thousand
shards of glass, the sparkling arc

of radioactive americium. At least
I'm patriotic, scarred and striped
acid red, and blue. I'm a medical miracle,

the most contaminated man on earth
who ever lived. No one
wants to shake my hand.

If the sun were the size of the sun,
my heart would be a baseball
in the steel and concrete isolation tank

at the edge of the hospital parking lot
I call home. I am a planet now—cragged
surface, magmatic core, and my nurses

might as well be astronauts.
I imagine under their space suits
they are beautiful. This half life

is lonely. My wife brings news and our dog
who doesn't know any better.
A few old friends shout greetings

through the door. If I have a superpower,
it might be clearing a room in seconds.
Or living 10,000 years, fading little by little.

RADIATION!

Invisible, tasteless, and odorless
    but sounds on certain tongues
like deep distrust
    of equations and lab coats
like panic wrapped for snacking
like the girl in Godzilla movies
    who can't run and scream at the same time
      who chooses screaming

THE VALUE OF GOOD DESIGN

The model is true to scale [she said].

This three-dimensional representation of a single-shell underground tank farm depicts a radioactive tank leak here [she was I, not schooled in the gray shades of public relations].

The cutaway view reveals a contamination plume [in a soothing color guaranteed not to dilate the eye] fixed hundreds of feet above ground water [she/I was green, maybe 24].

Most of the radiation [Did she neglect the critical questions? Did she even know what she didn't know?] is trapped in the unsaturated zone [Can you please confirm?], held in a matrix of silt and sand, though mathematical models predict [check this] some migration eventually to the river [according to documents and please verify, please answer the phone] in a matter of decades? measured in single years?] as accurate as the available data] Can you please confirm?].

The model demonstrates for the public eye there is no immediate danger of any kind.

AGAIN I'M ASKED IF I GLOW IN THE DARK

What glowed in childhood
was streetlight, moonlight,
the crack under my bedroom door, my
eyes, squeezed tight for a fireworks show.

Four houses up the street
Carolyn's mother could never sleep.
The blue flicker of Johnny Carson.
The bright lamp of her sewing machine.

Occasional headlights crawling across
my shelf of dolls. Their nonchalance.
The face in my poster of *Neuschwanstein*.
The face on the clock.

I revisit those nights at night, and the night
beyond me—the river, the trains, the dust—
revising my past. Enlightened.
So yes.

THE COLD WAR

It will turn quaint soon enough.
  Bomb shelters
already charm us, stuffed to their low ceilings

with batteries, board games and cans.
  Sardines are amusing,
and pineapple rings for dessert.

Old footage of duck-and-cover drills
  inspires us
to be world-weary and ironic,

to embrace the futile. Once we considered
  A-bombs big. Then H-bombs
exploded over the South Pacific.

We can laugh now
  at Khrushchev and his shoe,
beauty queens in radiation suits.

I'd wake bolt upright in my bed,
  afraid of a flash to come.
I'd buy books and extra spaghetti

to provide for our last days
  and pray that our end
be painless. I wasn't even that young.

I remember the red phone, and missile codes,
  how every movie hinged
on a clock ticking down.

We called it the arms race
  and there were two sides.
It was simple.

GOING DOWN

This is the guy in the white fastback Mustang
commuting to work on a Wednesday morning.

This is the woman with wooly blond hair
in the passenger seat of the white fastback car
who goes down on the man who is driving like hell,
passing a van, passing four cars, passing a bus on his way
to the job on a Tuesday or Wednesday morning.

These are the thousands who rise before dawn,
clip on their badges and climb on the bus,
or jump in their cars if they've got enough gas,
heading up north to their nut-numbing jobs,
when a Mustang swings past and a woman goes down
on a man growing famous for driving full-blown
into Monday, or Tuesday, morning.

This is a pattern of acting out
on the only road through the Hanford Works,
a.k.a. the ends of the earth,
entertaining the masses en route to the site
where they'll suit up in white, alert for alarms,
locked in a gate, protected by guards,
in a plant that makes high-grade plutonium stock
for government bombs to protect us from harm
on a typical Tuesday morning.

This is the landscape bleak and brown
that can hold its secrets for only so long
till they spill and spill, but for now and instead
the woman goes down on the man driving fast,
we cop our looks while they rocket past
and the rest of us feel . . . not closer to death, but further
from life as we slow at the gate for security check
on another Wednesday morning.

READING WELLS

between releasing a pebble to a deep well

and the distant plash rising up
to your ear

you accept all the mysteries
of water and geologic time

the inexorable
wearing down
bringing low everything
no matter everyone

and our mistakes

which are brutish
which will linger ten thousand years
which may end us altogether

one-thousand one
one-thousand two

are unforgiven
and unbounded

but pebble-size
compared with this keyhole view

on what can only be God
it is so deep and unlit

REDACTION III

As the industrial and public applications of AEC's future operations will be increasingly a public and not a secret matter, the sooner the present clumsy secrecy of Health Physics techniques is modified the better. —The Atomic Energy Commission, 1948

DEPOSITION

—On February 3, 2000, Hanford workers gathered at the request of Department of Energy headquarters to speak publicly about their health problems.

I wasn't there. I'd packed my car with houseplants
years ago, confident my rawhide neighbors would change

their campers' oil, mow and edge their lawns
like always, street after street of Hanford workers

who'd moved 30 years ago
from West Virginia or Pennsylvania or Tennessee

for a job—no saying what it was—for a pre-fab
landscaped with white rocks, for their kids

grown up like me, for their wives, hair freshly done,
comparing prices at Safeway. You know one

you know them all, I said at 25 and moved away,
brushed off the dust and breathed in the liberal city.

So I wasn't there when one by one they rose, walked stiffly
up the aisle in the Federal Building auditorium.

And yet I see them clearly, the same bastards
who grinned when schoolgirls strolled by, who flirted

with John Birch, and hunted pheasant, and owned
their stools at the cinderblock taverns downtown.

Whose sons and daughters would appear at school
sometimes with bruises on their arms.

Carolyn was there to testify and even she can't explain
how anybody there met anybody else's eyes.

It must have choked their throats like rotting meat,
admitting to cancers and hothouse-flower blood diseases,

each a different suffering. How did they stand on stage
and say what nobody could say aloud? And the ones

who came but couldn't speak. It's killing to think of
even now. Every one of them ashamed for falling ill

the way the anti-nuke fanatics said we would,
who've never known shit about anything,

who've never understood us and never will.

SONG OF THE SECRETARY, HOT LAB

All day in a concrete brick building without
even one shaft of natural light, I learned
to stare windows into my typing as my Selectric
raced along at 74 words per minute.

Atomic symbols—Sr-90, Cs-137, I-131,
U-238, Pu-239—darkened my work
like birds tangled in the sky. But I fixed on
clouds of my own bored making,

the small droplets of my idle thoughts,
and I floated among them, oblivious to birds . . .
while on the other side of the wall—
beyond the photo of my kids and dog

lined up in birthday hats—I don't know why
or when, a lab technician innocently moved
a very important brick,
and so a window opened over my desk,

though I never saw its light. All the same,
rays flooded in, and the shadow
of those birds darkened my dosimeter,
and later the mammogram of my right breast.

FLOW CHART

I

when Carolyn's father died
I drew a box around his death

and an arrow referencing
my America my

protective box
erected in the mind

this is how he died
chromosomal mutation
boiling his blood and marrow
exposure to radiation
an arrow   a flush of arrows

and this was a circle of lamplight
and Carolyn's grown voice on the phone

and the arrow circling back
to the box containing his death

containing a box
containing a box

II

Carolyn dumps out on her dining table
30 years of exposure documents

one man's official lifetime dose
painstakingly recorded

pencil dosimeter readings
whole-body counts in cramped cursive

radiation reported in units
that keep changing

we study a yellowing questionnaire
with boxes her father filled in

how many fish do you catch and eat each week?
where? what kind? do you hunt local game? local fowl?

yes   yes   too many   my god
pointing trigger fingers at our heads

charades for *shoot me now*

III

one box contains my childhood

the other contains his death

if one is true
how can the other be true?

I think at first I must choose
a box to believe in

but I'm all American

and lightning quick with the shell game

COYOTE

—Pronunciation: \ kī-ō'-tē, *chiefly Western* kī'-ōt \

After years away,
I met you again on the tongue
of an old friend from home. *Kī'-ōt.*

Trotting through sagebrush. Wild
by any name. I'd moved to a green isle city
that pronounced you *kī-ō'-tē*

and abandoned you by the side of the road.
I'd forgotten your silver, slope-shouldered form
and gaze.

You're not a citizen of language or memory,
but I am. Changing your name
was a betrayal of home

born of living among outsiders,
born of looking back through outsiders' eyes
at interchangeable houses landscaped

with wishing wells and pansies.
I could never love the brown hills around us.
Now, in the city, who can love the desert in me?

Kī'-ōt. Kī-ō'-tē. You live outside pronunciation.
I'm become like you
and can't say your name either way.

MUSEUM OF DOUBT

—Nagasaki photos

My love, allow yourself to stall, just a little,
  then enter the collection

          of black and white victims.
              Like inkblots
            they await your reply.

      Focus. I'm holding your hand.
              Their shadows

                on bridges and walls
            stop at 11:02

        like interrupted sundials.
                That, at least, you can respond to.

    You'll never make sense of rubble.
            The raw body proves difficult Braille.
        Illness you can fathom,
          with its slippers scuffing along a glassy hall.
                But can you feel it?

A kimono pattern imparted to the wearer's skin.

    Beloved, you've been carefully trained
            (do you sense your resistance?).

              Meaning is lost
        between the vulnerable eye
                and well-defended mind.

Who's on your side (you keep asking)?
                Not righteousness, not at this late hour?

      Look at you, unsure,
              but sure underneath.

DINNER WITH CAROLYN

Monterosso's is a railroad dining car
parked on a gravel lot with views
of a bank and the empty Payless
and the standard Richland tumbleweed tableau

Just before Dad died
he changed his mind about his life

They were swamped on a Thursday night
The waitress disappeared
forgot our meals
forgot to wipe up our spills

University doctors confirmed
his work at Hanford caused
chromosomal mutation
observed in Hiroshima victims
was due to
He would die
from radiation exposure

I imagined this was a train ride

Money was always
short on money

We drank wine
Remembered playing in Carolyn's room
the silk kimono from Korea

Money was always the last few dollars
He never said no

I ate capellini with prawns

He milled uranium slugs

Arranged prawn tails

He emptied train cars
down to the studs and floorboards
pegging the Geiger counter

That's where he found the praying mantis
he brought home

We drank wine
Imagined this was a train ride

Men came looking for "volunteers"
and offered to pay him extra
that meant the job was off-the record
hot
bad

It was twilight

He never said no I won't
to work nobody else would do

He called her Tootie
He took us camping in the Blues

The "volunteers" ran in and out
a minute or two at a time
everybody was scared
short on money
holding his breath

I remembered holding the praying mantis

He could have known his grandchildren
20 or 30 years

I remembered his Marines tattoo

The Hanford doctors told his lawyer
exposure to farm chemicals
as a youth

It was twilight
We imagined holding our breath

Dad said he'd trusted the wrong
people said he was safe

Forgot our meals

He gave his life
We won't take money
Money won't bring him back
He deserves a Medal of Honor from our country

Forgot to wipe up our spills

PORTRAIT OF MY FATHER

I conjure him after dinner, bent over
a pad of quadrille paper and the remnants

of a glass of wine. He pores over typed reports
and hand-scrawled formulas and marginalia.

The sun circles the birdfeeder, curtains open
and close against storms and careening stars,

his thin-striped tie grows paisley wide,
I dial his sideburns short to long to gray.

He faces north, plays Brahms and Mahler
on the record player. The atomic age blossoms

beyond the bank of backyard windows,
and here, on a regular night at home.

I can't know what he knew,
if a friend's or neighbor's or his own life-sum

ever appeared to him in a calculation.
But I do know what a man's life looked like,

how he'd rest his chin in his hand,
weigh a fact or theory, turn a page.

I will never feel so safe again.

MUSEUM OF A LOST AMERICA

I run a gloved hand over my country
    like a curator
        ready to frame what my mother and father passed down.

My country
    like bolts and bolts of fine-gauged fabric
                unfurled in the wind
        that never touched the weeds and dirt,
            not once.

        And I was possessive of it
    like mother love.
            Imagine owning in turn
            the four cardinal directions—
orchard in bloom;
            crickets at dark;
                    wheat up to the ridge;
                        fence line in snow.

Now I practice saying: *I've confused the landscape for my country*
    and my country for the landscape.

        And add it to my losses—

my sheeplike devotion to my shepherd
    that I've kept
        as long
            as I could.

My country of heroes.
Country of Lincoln.
        Country of fallen soldiers
    who didn't need to ask what America is.

Country of short memory,
          glass surfaces,
     and fingerprints easily wiped off.

Country of bombs bursting,
          anthems and fireworks,
               hand on my heart.

               Please advise, should I hang portraits
               of my mother and father in this hall?
               They're lost.
               They taught me this love.

               But how it would hurt them
          to see it soiled.

     I know somehow it's my failure, my fault
               that my own country betrayed me.

Oh Beautiful,
          I will not stop.
          I'll cling to any shred of America remaining,
               like a monkey
                    taken from her mother
               and clinging to a mother made of cloth.

IF YOU CAN READ THIS

[turn back]

[death] [horizon to horizon] [bedrock to sky]

[death] [river]   [indecipherable]

[death] [dust] [eyes]

[father and mother]   [love?] [indecipherable] [horizon to horizon]
    [bedrock to sky]

[plume/cloud]   [indecipherable]   [death] [blooming]   [generations]

[indecipherable]   [embrace (reaching out?)(pushing away?)]   [time passing]

[planet (or atom?)]

[traveler]   [death]   [turn back]

The 586-square-mile Hanford Site is located along the Columbia River in southeastern Washington State. A plutonium production complex with nine nuclear reactors and associated processing facilities, Hanford played a pivotal role in the nation's defense for more than 40 years, beginning in the 1940s with the Manhattan Project. Today, under the direction of the U.S. Department of Energy, Hanford is engaged in the world's largest environmental cleanup project, with a number of overlapping technical, political, regulatory, financial and cultural issues.

Physical challenges at the Hanford Site include more than 50 million gallons of high-level liquid waste in 177 underground storage tanks, 2,300 tons (2,100 metric tons) of spent nuclear fuel, 12 tons (11 metric tons) of plutonium in various forms, about 25 million cubic feet (750,000 cubic meters) of buried or stored solid waste, and about 270 billion gallons (a trillion liters) of groundwater contaminated above drinking water standards, spread out over about 80 square miles (208 square kilometers), more than 1,700 waste sites, and about 500 contaminated facilities.

—U.S. Department of Energy

NOTES

John Archibald Wheeler (1911–2008), eminent American theoretical physicist, interrupted his academic career to participate in the development of the atomic bomb at the Hanford Site. Even before the start-up of B Reactor, Wheeler had anticipated that the accumulation of "fission product poisons" would eventually impede the ongoing nuclear chain reaction by absorbing neutrons, and he correctly deduced (by calculating the half-life decay rates) that an isotope of xenon (Xe135) would be most responsible.

"A Great Physicist Recalls the Manhattan Project" closely adheres to an oral history provided by John A. Wheeler in *Working on the Bomb: An Oral History of WWII Hanford*, by S. L. Sanger (Portland, OR: Portland State University, 1995).

Enrico Fermi (1901–1954), Italian physicist, was a key developer of the first nuclear reactor at the University of Chicago, and he oversaw start-up of B Reactor at Hanford. Fermi was awarded the Nobel Prize in Physics in 1938 for his work on induced radioactivity and is regarded as one of the most important scientists of the twentieth century.

"Document Control" and "Bird's Eye View" are dedicated to Michele Stenehjem Gerber. The contamination referred to in "Herb Parker Feels Like Dancing" and "Bird's Eye View" is documented in Gerber's book, *On the Home Front: The Cold War Legacy of the Hanford Nuclear Site* (Lincoln: University of Nebraska Press, 1992, 1997, 2007). More generally, Gerber's book informs and inspires most of the poems in this collection.

Herbert Parker (1910–1984) began his career in England as a radiologist. At the start of World War II, he joined the Manhattan Project, first in Chicago, then Oak Ridge, and finally Richland, Washington, where he established the health physics program at the Hanford Engineer Works, a program that he directed until 1956 when he became overall manager for the Hanford Laboratories. Parker was instrumental in the development of the roentgen equivalent physical ("rep"), sometimes called the roentgen equivalent parker, and roentgen equivalent biological ("reb") units, predecessors to the rad and rem. He also established the first maximum permissible concentration for a radionuclide in air: $3.1 \times 10\text{-}11$ microcurie per cubic centimeter for Plutonium-239.

"Herb Parker Feels Like Dancing" is inspired in part by the recollections of

William J. Bair, PhD, who worked closely with and admired Herbert Parker. My thanks to Mr. Bair for the time he spent with me.

"Green Run" refers to the largest single known incident of atmospheric contamination in the history of the Hanford Site (Gerber, *On the Home Front*). Under the direction of the U.S. Air Force, 7,780 curies of Iodine-131 and 4,750 curies of Xenon-133 were intentionally released to the air on December 2–3, 1949. The experiment, which occurred two months after the detonation of the first Soviet atomic bomb, involved a processing "run" of uranium fuel that had been cooled for only a short time and was, therefore, "green." Much about the Green Run remains classified, but numerous clues indicate that America's Cold War scientists wanted to learn how to monitor Soviet nuclear weapon production by tracking iodine releases.

"Interlude for Dancers" is dedicated to dancers Nora Parkhurst, Lisa Peterson, and Paula Prewett; to teacher Lois Rathvon; and to Carolyn's daughter, Marisa.

The phrase "17,000 signs" referred to in "Augean Suite, Part II" was suggested by a communication from H. M. Parker to D. F. Shaw, "Control of Ground Contamination," August 19, 1954, on file as document HW-32808 in the U.S. Department of Energy Public Reading Room, library of Washington State University, Tri-Cities campus. "Augean Suite, Part III" is quoted entirely from that document.

"Augean Suite, Part V" includes in italics quotations from "Health Problems Associated with the Radiochemical Processing Industry," Herbert M. Parker, *A M A Archives of Industrial Health*, vol. 13, May 1956, which appears in *Herbert M. Parker: Publications and Other Contributions to Radiological and Health Physics*, edited by Ronald L. Kathren, Raymond W. Baalman, and William J. Bair (Columbus, OH: Battelle Press, 1986).

"Augean Suite, Part VI" is quoted entirely from the "Statement of Herbert M. Parker, Manager, Hanford Laboratories, General Electric, before the Subcommittee on Research, Development, and Radiation of the Joint Committee on Atomic Energy, Congress of the United States, June 1962," page 308, which appears in *Herbert M. Parker* (Columbus, OH: Battelle Press, 1986).

"Atomic Man" is based on Harold McCluskey, dubbed "The Atomic Man" when he survived a Hanford glove-box explosion in August 1976. McCluskey, at age sixty-four, received 500 times the occupational standard exposure limit of americium 241 and is considered the most radioactively contaminated human ever to survive. After five months of chelation therapy, McCluskey was released from steel-tank isolation and lived normally until his death at seventy-five from natural causes. There was no sign of cancer at his death (*Tri–City Herald*).

"The Value of Good Design" is set in the mid-1980s. By November 1997 the Department of Energy at Richland "confirmed that past leaks from Hanford's single shell tanks had reached groundwater in some cases and constituted 'a contributing source of groundwater contamination' beneath the site" (Gerber, *On the Home Front*).

"Reading Wells" references the more than 7,000 wells drilled on the Hanford Site to monitor groundwater contamination and movement, many to depths of 300 feet and deeper.

"Deposition" and "Song of the Secretary, Hot Lab" are based on testimony to the Department of Energy in a public hearing held in the Richland Federal Building Auditorium on February 3, 2000.

The U.S. Department of Energy site description on page 63 is reproduced from the Hanford Site Web page (www.Hanford.gov), where it appeared until 2010.

ACKNOWLEDGMENTS

My thanks to the editors of the following journals in which some of these poems first appeared, sometimes in slightly different forms:

5AM: "Map of Childhood," "To Carolyn's Father"
Adroit Journal: "The Cold War"
Center: "Interlude for Dancers"
DMQ Review: "Reading Wells," "Coyote," "Museum of Doubt"
High Desert Journal: "Siren Recognition," "Dinner with Carolyn"
The Iowa Review: "Bedroom Community," "Going Down," "Plume," "Song of the Secretary, Hot Lab," "Whole-Body Counter, Marcus Whitman Elementary"
Poetry Northwest: "Augean Suite"
Prairie Schooner: "Deposition," "Herb Parker Feels Like Dancing"
Solo Novo: "If You Can Read This"
The Southern Poetry Review: "Richland Dock, 1956," "Richland Dock, 2006"
Whitefish Review: "Green Run"
Willow Springs: "Mosquito Truck," "A Great Physicist Recalls the Manhattan Project"

A few of these poems were anthologized in the following volumes:

Don't Leave Hungry: Fifty Years of Southern Poetry Review (Fayetteville: University of Arkansas Press, 2009), "Richland Dock, 1956"
New Poets of the American West (Kalispell, MT: Many Voices Press, 2010), "Whole Body Counter, Marcus Whitman Elementary," "Going Down," and "Herb Parker Feels Like Dancing"
A Face to Meet the Faces: An Anthology of Contemporary Persona Poetry (Akron, OH: University of Akron Press, 2012), "A Great Physicist Recalls the Manhattan Project"
Ecopoetry: A Contemporary American Anthology (San Antonio, TX: Trinity University Press, 2012), "Plume" and "Green Run"
"Bedroom Community" appeared in an essay of the same name in *Poem Revised: 54 Poems, Revisions, Discussions* (Portland, OR: Marion Street Press, 2008).

The Peasandcues Press reprinted "Richland Dock, 2006" as a limited edition letterpress broadside.

My thanks to the National Endowment for the Arts for a 2005 Fellowship and to Artist Trust for a 2008 GAP Award. Thanks also to the Whiteley Center for time and space to write.

I am immensely grateful to Linda Bierds and University of Washington Press.

Michele Stenehjem Gerber's work has had a profound impact on our understanding of the Hanford Site. I am indebted to her for her time, honesty, and interest in mine.

For their frankness and encouragement at critical stages: Thanks to Dianne Aprile, Elizabeth Austen, Allen Braden, Fleda Brown, Jim Cihlar, T. Clear, Martha Collins, Jeff Crandall, Albert Goldbarth, Joseph and Marquita Green, David Hamilton, Holly Hughes, Kathryn Hunt, Lowell Jaeger, Tim Kelly, Judith Kitchen, Jared Leising, Marjorie Manwaring, Ted McMahon, Rosanne Olsen, Sylvia Pollack, Stan Rubin, Cody Walker, Gary Winans, and the Rainier Writers Workshop. I can never thank enough: Sharon Bryan, Jim Deatherage, Peter Pereira, Susan Rich. Alex, Tom, Elisabeth, and Steve Flenniken always. Thank you, dear Carolyn.

ABOUT THE POET

Kathleen Flenniken holds BS and MS degrees in civil engineering and spent eight years working as an engineer and hydrologist, three at the Hanford Nuclear Reservation in eastern Washington State. Her first collection of poems, *Famous*, won the 2005 Prairie Schooner Book Prize in Poetry and was named an ALA Notable Book and a finalist for the Washington State Book Award. Her poems have appeared in *The Iowa Review*, *Poetry*, *Poetry Daily*, and *The Southern Review*. She teaches poetry in the schools and is an editor with Floating Bridge Press, dedicated to publishing Washington State poets.

Photograph by Alexander Flenniken

A NOTE ON THE TYPE

The poems are set in 10.5 point Adobe Caslon with 15 point leading. Adobe Caslon is a modern revival based on English type designer William Caslon's original type specimens from the mid-1700s; it was created in 1990 by American type designer Carol Twombly for Adobe Systems. The poem titles are set in 14 point Ostrich Sans, a sans serif typeface created by American designer Tyler Finck in 2011. The typesetting is by Ashley Saleeba.

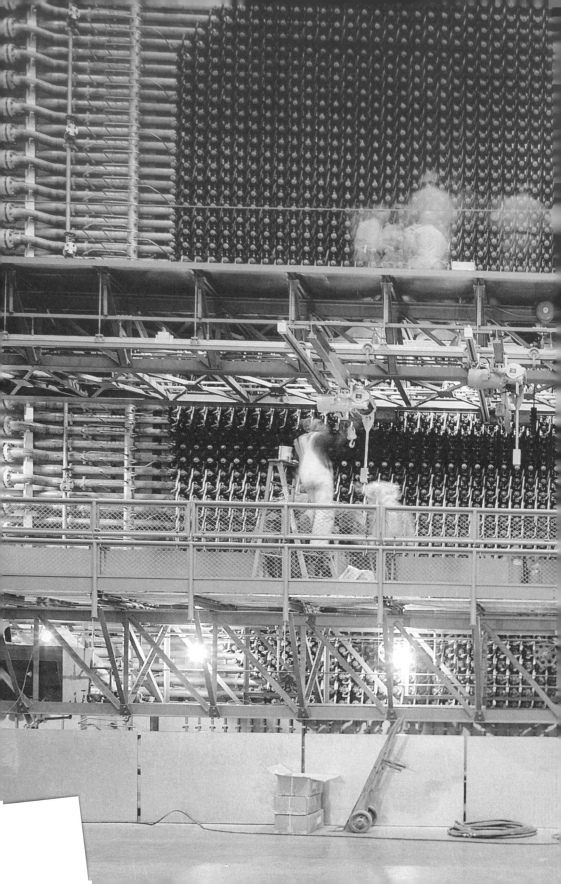